Plenty
Good Room

A Lenten Bible Study
Based on African American Spirituals

MARILYN E. THORNTON
WITH LEWIS V. BALDWIN

Abingdon Press
Nashville

PLENTY GOOD ROOM

A LENTEN BIBLE STUDY
BASED ON AFRICAN AMERICAN SPIRITUALS

ISBN: 978-1-501-82248-3

16 17 18 19 20 21 22 23 24 25 — 10 9 8 7 6 5 4 3 2 1

Manufactured in the United States of America

✳ Contents ✳

✳ Preface ✳

P*lenty Good Room: A Lenten Bible Study Based on African American Spirituals* utilizes spirituals from two earlier Bible study publications, *Plenty Good Room* (2002) and *On Ma Journey Now* (2005). It includes six spirituals: "Ev'ry Time I Feel the Spirit," "Jesus Walked This Lonesome Valley," "Po' Mou'ner's Got a Home at Last," "Plenty Good Room," "Ain't-a Dat Good News?" and "Were You There?" These songs were chosen from the earlier publications because the content of the lyrics lends itself as a guide through the Lenten season. The songs will aid participants in traveling with Jesus on his path to the cross. Using the lens of African American history and culture, these lessons move from the Day of Transfiguration (the Sunday before Lent), through the wilderness temptations, to the Last Supper and Good Friday.

While most of the lesson material for this edition is brand-new, some excerpts from the earlier *Plenty Good Room* are included. These choice selections, sometimes labeled "First Edition Notes," will be identified by the section title and page on which they are found in the first edition, written by Lewis Baldwin, Ph.D., Professor Emeritus in Religious Studies at Vanderbilt University. Baldwin is a preeminent scholar on the life and ministry of Martin Luther King Jr. He has published many titles, including *"Thou, Dear God": Prayers That Open Hearts and Spirits* (King Legacy, 2012) and *This Bright Light of Ours: Stories From the Voting Rights Fight*, with Maria Gitin (Modern South, 2014). He is also an expert on Spencer churches. His *Invisible Strands in African Methodism: History of the African Union Methodist Protestant and Union American Methodist Episcopal Churches, 1805–1980* (1983) is a study on the Mid-Atlantic Methodist denomination founded by Peter Spencer (1782–1843) in 1813.

Plenty Good Room: A Lenten Bible Study Based on African American Spirituals is not only the title of the study and the name of one of the spirituals used; it also reflects the reality that in God's kingdom, there is room for all, regardless of race, economic status, gender identity, ethnicity, or ability (Luke 14:12-13). In God's house there are many rooms (John 14:2). Through his saving work, Jesus has prepared a place for each one. Jesus has prepared a banquet table and set it with the Bread of Heaven and the Cup of Salvation, wrought from his own being. The season of Lent provides a space for us to better realize that not only is there room at the cross, there is plenty good room at the table and in the Kingdom, the place of God's transformational grace for all.

~Marilyn E. Thornton

✳ Introduction ✳

African American spirituals have been called the earliest sacred music of the United States. Although it is difficult to determine exactly when spirituals were created, historians agree that the birth of the spirituals coincided with the emerging days of slavery. Thousands of spirituals originated during the time of slavery, and, remarkably, these songs have been passed down from generation to generation.

The origin of the spirituals was influenced by many factors. First, slaves brought melodies, rhythms, and tones of music from their West African culture. This music was complex in beat, meter, and syncopation. The style also called for emotional improvisation, feeling, and expression in song.

Second, slaves were exposed to Christianity. Although they came to accept the same religion professed by the larger society, slaves were able to transcend some of the theological interpretations given to them, thereby grasping deep, spiritual truths.

Third, after combining musical form with words from the Bible and doctrines of the Christian faith, slaves added their own experience. Slaves in the United States experienced a horrible form of bondage and servitude. Although slavery is an ancient institution, slaves who came to the United States, to a degree not known in earlier times, were degraded, abused, and tortured for economic and political profit. The horror that the slaves endured seems almost unimaginable in contemporary times, and yet slavery in the United States is embedded firmly in our history. Remarkably, while the slaves suffered tremendous affliction and oppression, they were able to create exquisite songs of beauty, inspired by the power of God and the yearning for freedom. These songs, used by the slaves for comfort, encouragement, and healing, have now been bequeathed to us.

Slaves brought the African cultural tradition of applying music to every situation, from work routines to the naming of children. Every aspect of life was commemorated by song. Throughout history, this music has been called by many names, including jubilees, folk songs, shout songs, sorrow songs, slave songs, slave melodies, minstrel songs, and religious songs. And yet, because of the fervent passion and religious emotion of the songs, they became most commonly known as spirituals. The power of God's Holy Spirit, resonating with the spirits of all who sang them, created a notable intensity that often led to joyous shouts. Slaves were able to worship in the midst of their busy days by singing these songs, even when they were forbidden to attend church. Sung alone or in a group, the spirituals' power to heal, to soothe, and to strengthen made the music's impact a powerful testimony.

I'm gonna sing when the Spirit says sing,
I'm gonna sing when the Spirit says sing,
I'm gonna sing when the Spirit says sing,
And obey the Spirit of the Lord.

The world is indebted to the slaves—incredible, faith-filled saints—who survived this devastating period in history. These saints left behind music that has inspired millions, including the freedom fighters of the Civil Rights Movement in the 1960s. Like the generations before us, we are encouraged to pass on this beautiful, spirit-filled music to our descendants.

Plenty Good Room: A [Lenten] Bible Study Based on African American Spirituals provides an opportunity to reflect on the history and the context of the spirituals' origins. The accompanying CD [mp3 files] allows you to hear the songs' beautiful melodies and harmonies. Take the time to reflect on the sessions, the stories, the Bible readings, and the spirituals themselves in order to deepen your knowledge and understanding of the past and to hear the eternal truths of sacred word through song.

~Lewis V. Baldwin, from the first edition of *Plenty Good Room*

LESSON ONE

✳ Ev'ry Time I Feel the Spirit: A Mountaintop Experience ✳

BIBLE LESSON: Matthew 17:1-9

KEY VERSE: When they looked up, they saw no one except Jesus. (MATTHEW 17:8)

1 Six days later Jesus took Peter, James, and John his brother, and brought them to the top of a very high mountain. **2** He was transformed in front of them. His face shone like the sun, and his clothes became as white as light.

3 Moses and Elijah appeared to them, talking with Jesus. **4** Peter reacted to all of this by saying to Jesus, "Lord, it's good that we're here. If you want, I'll make three shrines: one for you, one for Moses, and one for Elijah."

5 While he was still speaking, look, a bright cloud overshadowed them. A voice from the cloud said, "This is my Son whom I dearly love. I am very pleased with him. Listen to him!" **6** Hearing this, the disciples fell on their faces, filled with awe.

7 But Jesus came and touched them. "Get up," he said. "Don't be afraid." **8** When they looked up, they saw no one except Jesus.

9 As they were coming down the mountain, Jesus commanded them, "Don't tell anybody about the vision until the Human One is raised from the dead."

"Ev'ry Time I Feel the Spirit"

Refrain:
Ev'ry time I feel the Spirit
Moving in my heart, I will pray. (2X)

Verse 1:
Upon the mountain my Lord spoke,
Out of his mouth came fire and smoke.
Looked all around me, looked so shine;
I asked my Lord if all was mine.

Verse 2:
Jordan River is chilly and cold,
Chills the body but not the soul.
There ain't but one train on this track,
Runs to heaven and right back.

Lenten Meditation

The season of Lent reminds the Christian disciple that Jesus' life was steeped in prayer and meditation. Throughout his life and particularly as he moved towards the cross (Matthew 16:21), Jesus took numerous opportunities to retreat. On at least one occasion, he and his disciples experienced a communal theophany, a visual and aural indication that they were in the presence of God, often called the Transfiguration. What a divine connection! High on a mountain, they saw a glorious vision. Everything was shining with God's glory, brilliant, dazzling white! They saw their ancestors, Elijah and Moses. They wanted to build structures for worship, but then God spoke. They were not ready and quivered in fear. When they returned to the community, after a failed healing attempt (Matthew 17:14-21), Jesus told his disciples that some things only happen through much prayer and fasting. [1] As we pray through this season, let us envision the ministry Jesus has for us, understanding that we are building the kingdom as God wills, not as we will.

Prayer
Be thou my vision, dear Lord. May your will be done on earth as it is in heaven. Amen.

First Edition Notes
"Rock of One's Soul," pages 10–11

Many spirituals reflected the slaves' sense of self-worth in the face of an unjust system that questioned and violated their humanity. A major belief in society was that slaves had no souls; they were viewed as slightly above animals. In the minds of some slave owners and many others of European descent, this belief justified the slaves' subhuman treatment. Yet the slaves believed they did have souls and, furthermore, that their souls were intimately connected to God.

Slaves knew from deep inside their beings that within their souls was the life and vitality stemming from the presence of God's Spirit and that this Spirit moved within. This was a Spirit they could feel! One of the reasons worship was so popular with the slaves, even after days of hard, draining work, was that the activities of praise and worship confirmed that they were alive and connected to the Divine.

Place and Time (Matthew 17:1)

Thus far, despite Peter's declaration that Jesus was the Messiah, the Son of the living God (Matthew 16:16), Jesus was not all that different from the regular traveling prophets and preachers that the Hebrew children had experienced throughout their history, with miraculous feedings and healings, great sermons, and even resurrections. This is what it meant to be a great prophet. But Jesus was more, and they had come to the time and place for this revelation, the time and place that would reveal what it meant to be so intimately connected with him—that they must take up a cross as he must take up a cross (16:24), and that their perspective must mirror his vision.

Six days after Jesus tells them that some of them would see the glory of God's kingdom (Matthew 16:27-28), he takes Peter, James, and John to a high mountain. No one else was with them. Rather than praying alone (Luke 6:12-13; Mark 1:35) or sending all of the disciples away (Matthew 14:21-23), at this time and place, Jesus takes three disciples with him. They had to do what he was doing and see what he would see.

Discussion Point
What is a theophany?

Theophany, Part I: What Did They See? (Matthew 17:2-4)

What the disciples saw was their friend and rabbi, Jesus, changed in appearance before their very eyes! His face was shining like the sun from which one must shield one's eyes. He "looked so shine," even his clothes shimmered in a white light, his entire being covered in transcendent, divine glory. They saw Jesus, not just a regular itinerant prophet, not just a healer or teacher, not just Mary's baby; but they saw Deity, a glorified being, God!

And they also saw Moses and Elijah.

Like Moses, the Lawgiver, who had met God on Mount Sinai and set the foundation for what it meant to be a prophet, Peter, James, and John had the privilege of seeing the glorified face of God.

No prophet like Moses has yet emerged in Israel; Moses
knew the LORD face-to-face! That's not even to mention
all those signs and wonders that the LORD sent Moses to do
in Egypt—to Pharaoh, to all his servants, and to his entire
land. (Deuteronomy 34:10-11)

And then there was Elijah. Elijah also met God on Mount Horeb, instructed
by God to "go out and stand at the mountain before the LORD. The LORD is
passing by." After experiencing a mighty wind, an earthquake, and a fire, God
spoke to Elijah in the silence (1 Kings 19:11-12).

Neither of these prophets had seen death in a conventional way. Elijah
was carried off alive in a whirlwind by a flaming chariot drawn by horses
of fire (2 Kings 2:11). Moses had been laid to rest by God's own self in the
land of Moab (Deuteronomy 34:1-6). Yet here they were, recognizable to
the disciples, talking with Jesus, clear evidence that there is life after death.
Perhaps they were discussing how the circumstances around Jesus' death
would be so unconventional that it would result in making eternal life
available to all.

The first to gather his wits, Peter proposed to build a dwelling, designed
for worship as in God's tabernacle (Exodus 40:34) or like those used during
Jewish festivals. However, as he spoke something else happened!

Discussion Point
Speak to the importance of Moses and Elijah.

Theophany, Part II: What Did They Hear?
(Matthew 17:5)

What they heard was a voice coming out of the cloud that overshadowed
them. "Upon the mountain my Lord spoke. Out of his mouth came fire
and smoke!" It was a bright cloud as in the days when God led the Hebrew
children out of Egypt in a cloudy pillar of fire and smoke. The voice spoke
plainly and clearly, "This is my Son whom I dearly love. I am very pleased
with him. Listen to him!" It was none other than the voice of God, whose
three-part announcement accomplished a number of things:

1. The disciples knew who Elijah and Moses were. They understood
   their role in the relationship the people had with God. They were just
   beginning to understand who Jesus was. According to the voice of God,
   Jesus was greater than the greatest of Hebrew prophets. He was the Son

of God. God was his Father in a way that was different from the rest of humanity.

2. The voice let the disciples know that Jesus the Son was loved by God, who was pleased with him. Family love is not automatic, nor is paternal favor. Even as sonship is an elevated patriarchal status, from Isaac/Jacob/Esau to David/Adonijah/Absalom, the biblical record is full of stories of family treachery. For God to claim Jesus as Son, the Beloved, with whom God was well pleased, was significant and purposeful.

3. The voice told the disciples to listen to Jesus and follow his teaching. Hebrew culture at that time was still mostly an oral tradition with knowledge passed down by word of mouth. This is why Jesus often prefaced his teaching with, "You have heard . . . ," something in relationship to the law of Moses (Matthew 5:21-22, 27-30, 38-39). His teaching often pushed the envelope on what they had been practicing for centuries. The Law was perfected in the teachings of Jesus. God's command for the disciples to "listen to Jesus" echoed the Shema:

> Israel, listen! Our God is the LORD! Only the LORD! Love the LORD your God with all your heart, all your being, and all your strength. These words that I am commanding you today must always be on your minds. (Deuteronomy 6:4-6)

Just as they obeyed the law of Moses, now they were to obey Jesus.

Listening is not just about the physical ability to hear. Listening means to take into one's heart and mind what another is saying and to act accordingly. Loving Jesus means to obey his commands. And he only gave one—that we should love one another.

Discussion Point
What are three points made by God in this encounter?

Theophany, Part III: What Did They Do? (Matthew 17:6-8)

Peter, James, and John seemed to take the presence of these long-gone ancestors (some might say ghosts) in stride. Perhaps it is because their worldview was similar to an African worldview that the departed remained intimately connected with the living as part of their daily existence. The ancestors have a double existence; they are with God in a spirit world *and* among the people, watching over them and protecting them. As Lewis Baldwin writes in the first edition of *Plenty Good Room*, "The African worldview affirmed the sacred world as thoroughly enmeshed and central to all aspects of life. God was everywhere and experienced in all things" (page 34).

Nevertheless, upon hearing the voice of God, the disciples were filled with fear. Fear was common to people who experienced God's presence so abruptly: the father of John the Baptist, Zechariah (Luke 1:11-12); the shepherds at Jesus' birth (Luke 2:9). It is an unpleasant emotion caused by a sense that danger, pain, and/or threat is near. As did the Roman soldiers who were confronted when the angel of the Lord rolled away the stone of Jesus' tomb, the disciples fell down, overcome with fear (Matthew 28:4).

Jesus' response was a God response: comfort and assurance. He moves away from his heavenly companions to be close to his earthly ones, touching them, encouraging them to get up! Jesus is right there. There is no need for fear. And when they look up, they see only Jesus: their rabbi, leader, healer, and friend. Jesus remains as the abiding presence of God, a presence that "soothes our doubts and calms our fears," and empowers us to get up and do what has to be done.

Discussion Point
What causes you fear?

Coming Down the Mountain (Matthew 17:9)

What goes up must come down. Coming down from a high time may provide an opportunity to debrief and to share what has happened, an examination of life-changing experiences. But Jesus instructs Peter, James, and John that what happened on the mountain is between him and them, not to be discussed even with the other disciples. Having had an out-of-mind, out-of-body experience, in which the mundane things of life had been suspended, time and place once again become important.

Lent is a time when certain mundane things are suspended. We may eat less, take more time to pray and to meditate, spend more time in sacred spaces. It is a time when we may experience the abiding presence of God in a special way. Like the Transfiguration, however, we cannot stay in the moment.

Transfiguration events inform and facilitate our transformation into more disciplined and empowered followers of Christ. They are meant to help us remember to pray every time we feel the Spirit and that feeling the Spirit is necessary for true discipleship. They are meant to prepare us for the work ahead: the work of listening to Jesus, the imaginative exertion to continue to see the sacred once we get to the foot of the mountain, the challenge not to bend down in fear as we encounter the low places and valleys of life. They are for the purpose of moving us to be as fully human as Jesus, the Human One, and connecting us with the divinity placed in us by Creator God.

The Lenten journey begins at the top of a mountain but is informed by the time and place of Jesus' crucifixion and resurrection, the good news, which for the Christian disciple gives meaning to all of life.

Discussion Point
After a mountaintop experience, what aspects of transformation did you gain?

1. After the Transfiguration event, a man brought his epileptic child to Jesus. He had already taken him to the disciples, but they were unable to heal him. Jesus determined that the disciples did not have enough faith. Some biblical editions also include that the kind of faith they needed would come through fasting and prayer.

LESSON TWO

✳ This Lonesome Valley: A Time of Temptation ✳

BIBLE LESSON: Matthew 4:1-4

KEY VERSE: Jesus replied, "It's written, *People won't live only by bread, but by every word spoken by God.*" (MATTHEW 4:4)

1 Then the Spirit led Jesus up into the wilderness so that the devil might tempt him. 2 After Jesus had fasted for forty days and forty nights, he was starving. 3 The tempter came to him and said, "Since you are God's Son, command these stones to become bread."

4 Jesus replied, "It's written, *People won't live only by bread, but by every word spoken by God.*"

"Jesus Walked This Lonesome Valley"

Verse 1:
Jesus walked this lonesome valley.
He had to walk it by himself.
Oh, nobody else could walk it for him.
He had to walk it by himself.

Verse 2:
I must walk this lonesome valley. I have to walk it
*   by myself. Oh, . . .*

Verse 3:
We must walk this lonesome valley. We have to walk . . .

Lenten Meditation

Life contains its lonesome valleys: times when you hit bottom, when you go so low, you can go no lower, times when you feel as alone as alone can be, with no shoulder to cry on and no one to hold your hand. Indeed, there are experiences that, despite your preference, you cannot avoid; no one else can take your place. You have to do it, nobody else.

Geographically, *valleys* are elongated depressions between hills or mountains or flat, low regions drained by river systems. Figuratively, they may be periods or situations that are filled with fear or gloom such as "the valley of the shadow of death" (Psalm 23:4, KJV). Jesus, like all of humanity, had his "lonesome valley" moments. He was actually guided into this one by the Holy Spirit. And though he was physically weakened and bereft of human companionship, God's Word accompanied him in his heart. During this Lenten season, let us take opportunities to hide God's Word in our hearts. God's Word will ready us for lonesome valley moments and remind us that God's hand and shoulder are always available.

Prayer

Thank you, God, for your presence in every situation. Even when I walk through the darkest valley, I fear no danger because you are with me; in Jesus' name. Amen.

First Edition Notes
"Escape and Deliverance From Slavery," page 15

Escaping slaves traveled through dangerous territory, hid in swamps from bounty hunters, and ran from wild animals. Runaway slaves typically traveled by foot at night and slept during the day. Often, slaves would hide in the homes or on the property of kind people who would provide them with food, clothing, and medical assistance. A large number of persons who aided slaves on the Underground Railroad were white and belonged to religious groups such as the Methodists and the Quakers. Houses and other places in which slaves were allowed to hide were called "stations" because they were the stops slaves would make while traveling on the "train." Singing must have helped to inspire the slaves with a sense of divine sanction for their escape. They believed that God wanted them to be free; and the holy, authoritative sound of the song encouraged that faith.

Into the Wilderness (Matthew 4:1)

Another song in the Negro spiritual tradition asks the question,

> *Tell me, how did you feel when you come out de wilderness,*
> *Come out de wilderness, come out de wilderness?*
> *How did you feel when you come out de wilderness,*
> *Leanin' on the Lord?*

In order to come out of the wilderness, you had to have gone into the wilderness—a dry, unfriendly place—where it may appear that God has not touched at all. Indeed, the Hebrew word for "wilderness" or "desert" is *midbar*, meaning "without word," either a place that bears no description or a place where no other human voice can be heard.

The Middle Passage was a wilderness and a lonesome valley for Africans stolen from their homelands and transported into chattel slavery. The bottom of those ships where they lay was indescribably horrible! The captured listened for voices they could understand but had been deliberately separated into different language and cultural groups. Just as immigrants from Mexico or Syria cross borders into desert lands, escaping slaves went into the wilderness of swamps and unknown territories in order to come out of the moral wasteland of slavery. Wilderness places represent the valleys of life, and Jesus, as any human being, had to go into the wilderness.

His wilderness experience parallels that of the Hebrew children in Exodus. They were led into the wilderness in order to continue a relationship with the God of their ancestors. "After you bring the people out of Egypt, you will come back here and worship God on this mountain" (Exodus 3:12). And it is often the case that we must go into a place where no human voice can be heard in order to hear the voice of God.

Jesus, however, was being led by God's Spirit into the wilderness for the purpose of being tempted by the devil. The ultimate purpose was for Jesus, the Human One, to become mature in his bond with his heavenly Father even as he journeyed on earth; that he would be able to withstand the trials of earthly living. His experience serves as an example on how to come out of the wilderness, intact and complete.

> My brothers and sisters, think of the various tests you encounter as occasions for joy. After all, you know that the testing of your faith produces endurance. Let this endurance complete its work so that you may be fully mature, complete, and lacking in nothing. (James 1:2-4)

When we pray in the Lord's Prayer not to be led into temptation, it is like asking God to be a hedge between selfish desires and human foibles.

> No one who is tested should say, "God is tempting me!" This is because God is not tempted by any form of evil, nor does he tempt anyone. Everyone is tempted by their own cravings; they are lured away and enticed by them.
> (James 1:13-14)

Jesus was led into the wilderness by the Holy Spirit, but he was tempted by the devil, who used what human beings desire—food, position, and power—in a series of tests.

Discussion Point
What temptations signal that you need to grow spiritually?

Forty Days and Forty Nights (Matthew 4:2)

To *fast* means to abstain from food and (often) drink for a certain length of time, directing one's focus away from everyday tasks and toward God. Fasting requires discipline and self-control. In the wilderness, Jesus fasted for forty days and forty nights.

From the days of Noah, the number forty and the time span of forty days and forty nights have had religious and cultural importance. "It rained on the earth forty days and forty nights" (Genesis 7:12). An old African American quartet song "Didn't It Rain?" retells Noah's story:

> *Didn't it rain? Didn't it rain? Oh my Lord, didn't it rain? (2X)*
> *It rained forty days and nights without stopping.*
> *Noah was glad when the rain stopped dropping.*
> *When I get to heaven gonna put on my shoes,*
> *Walk around glory and spread the news!*

Bernard Roth wrote the classic blues song "Forty Days and Forty Nights," which was first recorded by blues great Muddy Waters in 1956. The lyrics borrow this biblical timing to express sorrow over love gone wrong. "Forty days and forty nights since my baby left this town." He describes how although the sun is shining, it is as if it were raining because she has broken his heart. He has been crying for "forty days and forty nights like a ship out on the sea."[1] The singer prays for his time without her to be over, that this woman will come home. He was experiencing a wilderness and a lonesome valley without her!

The Hebrew children wandered in the wilderness for forty years. This wandering was a punishment, providing time for those who had refused to trust God and been disobedient after the miraculous deliverance from Egypt to pass away (Joshua 5:6). It was also a time that helped the people to form a bond of trust with God, who provided all that they needed during those forty years of wandering (Deuteronomy 2:7).

The period of Lent is forty days from Ash Wednesday to Holy Saturday (the day before Easter). The count does not include Sundays. Why is Sunday not in the forty-day count for Lent? Every Sunday is a day of celebrating the Resurrection, no fasting or mourning on Sunday. Enslaved black people had a belief that when we get to heaven, every day will be Sunday: a gathering of the saints, no work, plenty of food, and praising God all day! During this time, let us take an opportunity to bond more closely with God, who loves us and provides every need.

Discussion Point
How does the season of Lent impact your life?

The First Temptation (Matthew 4:3)

After fasting for forty days and nights, Jesus was famished. He was in a valley of hunger, a personal food desert. Hunger has driven people to steal, to kill, to say things they would never say. Hunger prevents children from learning. Valleys, wildernesses, and deserts represent opportunities for the devil. He was quick to take advantage of Jesus in his lack, tempting him on a couple of levels:

1. Challenging his status as God's Son
2. Challenging his power as Creator

Just forty days before, at Jesus' baptism, God had confirmed Jesus' status as the Son (Matthew 3:13-17). Yet the devil is always vying for position, throwing shade (signifying) and creating doubt. The KJV and the NIV Bibles translate the CEB "since" in Matthew 4:3 as "if," which is a conjunction introducing a conditional clause. It introduces a hypothetical situation, that something *might* be possible, not a certainty. The word *if* is designed to challenge, to force Jesus to prove something he does not have to prove. But it does not end there. The devil, in a competitive spirit, tells Jesus what he needs to do in order to prove that he is indeed the Word of God (John 1:1-3), that is—to create something, bread from stones.

There are communities in our cities that are called food deserts, indicating places where fresh foods (whole fruit, grains and vegetables, fresh meat) are unavailable, while fast foods and sodium- and sugar-filled "foods" are plentiful. The people are receiving stones instead of appropriate nourishment. Food deserts contribute to the high rate of obesity among black children as well as the high rates of diabetes and hypertension among black adults. The lack of affordable transportation intersects with the presence of food deserts. There is no way to get to the places where more healthful foods are sold. And with no car, there is only so much one can carry in one's hands on a bus or train as well as the time factor. Economics further intersects with the presence of food deserts. Bad food is cheap, while more healthful choices cost significantly more.

As followers of Jesus, who as part of his earthly ministry fed and ate with people, preached about a heavenly banquet, and provided the spiritual food for our salvation, we must raise our consciousness concerning this issue. Many of our churches reside in food deserts. What is your church doing to challenge the path to bad health so many in our communities are destined to take?

> Imagine a brother or sister who is naked and never has enough food to eat. What if one of you said, "Go in peace! Stay warm! Have a nice meal!"? What good is it if you don't actually give them what their body needs? In the same way, faith is dead when it doesn't result in faithful activity.
>
> (James 2:15-17)

Jesus did not have to prove himself by changing stones into bread. However, as his followers, part of our mission is getting people what their bodies need.

Discussion Point
What can be done about food deserts?

Jesus' Response (Matthew 4:4)

Jesus understood the devil's role as prosecutor, one charged with finding wrongdoing and guilt (Job 2:1-2). He was secure in his status as God's Son and had hidden God's Instruction in his heart. Food for the body is necessary, but if our motives and desires are wrong, once strengthened, we may still make wrong choices. The true test is making right choices even in our weakness.

We love to quote Jesus and say, "The spirit is eager [willing], but the flesh is weak" (Matthew 26:41b), ignoring his preface, "Stay alert and pray so that you won't give in to temptation" (41a). Jesus has demonstrated that we do not have to give in! With songs, Bible passages, prayer, and community, we have the spiritual resources available to overcome temptation.

I remember a time when my family was flung into a lonesome valley of church dysfunction. It was a traumatic event from which children needed to be shielded. We did not live close to any biological family and did not know who to trust in our church family. However, there was a woman who lived in another town and was not privy to local church issues, and with whom I'd had discussions about prayer and faith. After I received the call concerning the problem, my mind was filled with confusion. I called her, and her prayer strengthened me to be able to discern the first step in moving through and out of our wilderness. Then I called a neighbor, also not connected to local church politics, and her family lovingly took care of our children, freeing their parents to begin that lonesome walk and realize that Jesus was walking with us.

Church dysfunction tempts people to leave the church. It is especially hard on the spiritually immature. But we can come out of any wilderness. We must remember that we do not live by bread alone but by every word that comes from the mouth of God. That word is found by the power of the Holy Spirit in community, in the Bible, in song, in prayer, and in the very person of Jesus Christ, the bread of life (John 6:35).

This Lenten season, take the time to strengthen your spiritual resources, the things that feed your spirit, and your relationship with Jesus. And then when you are asked, "Tell me, how did you feel when you came out of the wilderness?" you will be able to say, "It can only be done by leaning on the Lord!"

Discussion Point
How did you feel when you came out of a wilderness experience?

1. Written by Bernard Roth. Lyrics © Sunflower Music Incorporated. See *http://www. metrolyrics.com/forty-days-forty-nights-lyrics-muddy-waters.html*.

LESSON THREE
✳ Bow Down on Your Knees:
A Time of Repentance ✳

BIBLE LESSON: Matthew 4:5-11

KEY VERSE: The devil left him, and angels came and took care of him.
(MATTHEW 4:11)

5 After that the devil brought him into the holy city and stood him at the highest point of the temple. He said to him, **6** "Since you are God's Son, throw yourself down; for it is written, *I will command my angels concerning you, and they will take you up in their hands so that you won't hit your foot on a stone.*"

7 Jesus replied, "Again it's written, *Don't test the Lord your God.*"

8 Then the devil brought him to a very high mountain and showed him all the kingdoms of the world and their glory. **9** He said, "I'll give you all these if you bow down and worship me."

10 Jesus responded, "Go away, Satan, because it's written, *You will worship the Lord your God and serve only him.*" **11** The devil left him, and angels came and took care of him.

"Po' Mou'ner's Got a Home at Last"

Refrain:
No harm, no harm, go tell Brother Elijah,
No harm, no harm, po' mou'ner's got a home at last.

Verse 1:
Mou'ner, mou'ner, ain't you tired o' mou'nin'?
Bow down on your knees and pray.
Mou'ner, mou'ner, ain't you tired o' mou'nin'?
J'ine (join) de band with the angels.

Verse 2:
Sinner, sinner, ain't you tired o' sinnin'?

Verse 3:
Gambler, gambler, ain't you tired o' gamblin'?

Lenten Meditation

"All night, all day, angels watchin' over me, my Lord." This phrase from another Negro spiritual is played out in today's lesson. Jesus has been fasting. Depleted physically, emotionally, and spiritually from his battle with the enemy, he receives a band of angels who wait on him. Conventional wisdom and biblical literature demonstrate that angels bring messages from God. Mary receives the message of her pregnancy from the angel Gabriel (Luke 1: 26-38). As Jacob flees his brother, upon laying his head on a rock to sleep, he dreams about angels ascending and descending a ladder to heaven. When he awakens, he knows that he has been in the presence of God (Genesis 28:10-17).

Often when we are between a rock and a hard place, we experience God's presence in human angels who come by to bring a plate of food, a word of encouragement, or to pray or minister to our physical needs. During this Lenten season, let us find ways to be angels of mercy to someone who is struggling. May our presence be the message from heaven that will draw someone to journey with Jesus Christ.

Prayer

Dear Lord, I'm tired of mou'nin'. As I bow down on my knees, I ask for you to send an angel *my* way. Allow *me* to be part of that heavenly band that will bring a message of hope to someone else; in Jesus' name. Amen.

First Edition Notes
"Slavery's Balm for Weary Souls," page 22

The testimony of the spirituals indicates that slaves were strengthened by the power of God that came from within. Although many slaves attended church with their masters, heard evangelists, and attended camp meetings and revivals, it was the testimony burning within their hearts that gave them the strength to hold on. Inspired by the gospel fundamentals to which they were exposed, slaves were able to transform and redefine their understanding of the Christian faith. The slave community appropriated religion through the teachings of Christ and the Old Testament stories, finding the true meaning of the gospel.

The Pinnacle of the Temple (Matthew 4:5)

When we are in the valleys and wildernesses of life, we long for success and times of celebration. And yet, it is often at those high times and pinnacles of success that we find ourselves being tempted the most. Perhaps we even forget how we got there, thinking that it was all of our own effort. We forget the angels along the way who gave us a helping hand and begin to say we pulled ourselves up by our own bootstraps.

Too many times we have heard stories of how sports stars, entertainers, and even ministers have reached a high point in their careers or public life only to be brought down by some egregious act of sin: gambling debts, sexual misconduct, pathological lying. They may feel that they are too big to fail or that they are now able to do whatever they want. Or, as shown in the old-style cartoons, they begin to listen more intently to the demon on one shoulder than to the angel on the other side. They forget that "pride goes before a fall."

Scripture shows us that Jesus, too, had to contend with this temptation. The enemy took him to the highest point of the Temple—the Temple that was built to honor God, the Temple where the people brought their offerings to the Lord, the Temple whose dimensions had been proscribed by God for the glory of God. The devil, who represented the very antithesis of God's glory, brought Jesus to the pinnacle of the Temple and gave him not just a challenge but a dare, his second temptation.

Discussion Point
Think about some of the high points in your life. Why are they so hard to maintain?

If You Are: The Second Temptation (Matthew 4:6)

It was a dare that was wrapped up in the identity of who Jesus was. Yes, Jesus was the Son of God. God had just opened the heavens and announced this to the world when Jesus was baptized (Matthew 3:13-17). But Jesus had also been born of a woman; he was the Son of Man, the Human One. His divinity was embodied in the flesh with all of its frailties. Appealing to human pride, the devil dared him to prove that even as being fully human, he was still indeed fully divine.

Wars have been started on dares, especially ones that question a person's parentage or the validity of a parent's power. "My daddy is bigger and better than yours. He's got a bigger car, a better job, more money!" And in the black community, don't start talking about somebody's mama! There is an entire oral tradition, playing the dozens, built upon proving that one's mama is better than the other's. Unfortunately, this is done by putting down women: saying nasty and ugly things about another's mother in order to keep the upper hand. Again, the ultimate result is a fight on the playground, in the schoolyard, in the alley.

The devil was basically challenging Jesus to a game of the dozens: "If you are God's Son, God will save you when you throw yourself off of this high point. After all, this is God's Temple. God is not going to allow this kind of dishonor to happen. God is not going to let you commit suicide or even hurt your foot! Just as you are almost to the ground, angels will come to your rescue."

As Jesus stood with the enemy at the top of the Temple dedicated to his Father, I can imagine a crowd of the devil's minions crying out, "Jump! JUMP!" "Do it, Jesus!"

Discussion Point
Why do people egg on risky behavior?

Jesus' Response: Risky Behavior (Matthew 4:7)

As with the first temptation, Jesus' response to his current situation was informed by the words of the Hebrew Bible in Deuteronomy 6:16: Don't test God! His answer points to God's sovereign and independent will. God's decisions are not based on what the current circumstance might be, but on God's eternal omniscience. As Isaiah said, "For my thoughts are not your thoughts, nor are your ways my ways, says the Lord. For as the heavens are higher than the earth, so are my ways higher than your ways and my thoughts than your thoughts" (Isaiah 55:8-9, NRSV). Jesus' answer reflects his perfect knowledge of God.

It is not our job to try to force God's hand or to prove God's power by participating in risky behavior. It is ridiculous for a person to purposefully throw one's self in front of an oncoming bus and expect not to be physically obliterated. On this earth, we live by the laws of nature, laws of science already put in place by God who created all things. To test these laws by refusing to use a seatbelt, or drinking while driving, or taking unnecessary risks is to put God to the test, trying to make God prove God's power. God ain't got time for that! And neither do the people you love and who love you. While survival of risky behavior is surely a sign of God's grace, we would do better to show God's love by avoiding risky behavior. Only God has any idea of how the outcome, whatever it may be, will be woven into God's eternal plan for humanity.

Discussion Point
How did you feel upon surviving a foolish action?

The Third Temptation: Higher Heights (Matthew 3:8-10)

The devil must have known some of the proverbs we use: "If at first you don't succeed, try, try again!" or "The third time's a charm!" He was determined to usurp Jesus' status as the one and only beloved Son of God. So he took Jesus up higher than the mount upon which the Temple stood. He took Jesus to a place where he could see all the beautiful cities of the earth. As if he owned it, liar that he is, the enemy offered to Jesus the entire world if he would bow down and worship him.

Those Hebrew boys Shadrach, Meshach, and Abednego had faced a similar proposition. They chose not to bow down to the golden idol upon hearing the music of the horn, pipe, lyre, harp, and drum. They refused to dance to the king's tune. And they told the infuriated King Nebuchadnezzar of their decision to his face:

> If our God—the one we serve—is able to rescue us from the furnace of flaming fire and from your power, Your Majesty, then let him rescue us. But if he doesn't, know this for certain, Your Majesty: we will never serve your gods or worship the gold statue you've set up. (Daniel 3:17-18)

Nebuchadnezzar ordered them to be tied up and thrown into a furnace that burned more hotly than ever before. But immediately, God was with them in the furnace where they walked around freely.

African Americans, whether slave or free, have faced similar circumstances. They could believe what those in charge want them to believe or they could reappropriate what was being taught and transform and redefine their understanding of who they were/are as children of God. Prophetic faith is one that promotes a radically different vision of the world we see now. The devil's view was too limited. Jesus, the Word of God, had already participated in the creation of the universe (Genesis 1:3, 26; John 1:1-5).

The "triple prong sickness . . . of racism, excessive materialism, and militarism"[1] identified by Martin Luther King Jr. in 1967 has always been around. Like the black slave, those Hebrew boys were being taught that their culture was worthless (Daniel 1:1-4). Even today, America teaches that it, and not God, is the only superpower. Even as the modern capitalist system was built on the backs of people of African descent (insurance companies, banks, agriculture, trade), bowing down to the golden idol remains a temptation for all people, including blacks.

Prophetic faith that proclaims a different perspective—good news for the poor, the disinherited, and the oppressed; freedom for the imprisoned and enslaved; and sight for the blind—requires a view from higher heights that only the God of the universe is able to provide (Luke 4:18; Amos 5:14-15, 23-24).

Discussion Point
Why is it important to maintain a vision of the world as God would have it?

The Devil Left (Matthew 3:11)

As we travel with Jesus on this Lenten journey, let us bow down on our knees to the only one who can save us from temptation, whatever it may be. God will meet us in whatever fiery furnace that threatens to consume our faith and help us to find the true meaning of the gospel message. When we call on the name of Jesus, the devil can do nothing; he must depart, and "the world can't do us no harm." We can walk around freely as our ever-present angels watch over and minister to us. When we quit our moaning and mourning about what the devil is doing, we can be strengthened by God's power and become angels that bring hope and help to a hurting world.

Discussion Point
How can you be an angel to someone this week?

1. From "The Three Evils of Society," a speech by Dr. Martin Luther King Jr., delivered on August 31, 1967, at the National Conference on New Politics in Chicago, Illinois. See *https://connectere.wordpress.com/2016/01/19/the-three-evils-address-delivered-by-martin-luther-king-8311967/* and *http://www.thekingcenter.org/king-philosophy*.

LESSON FOUR
✳ Plenty Good Room:
Preparing the Guest Room ✳

BIBLE LESSON: Mark 14:10-26

KEY VERSE: I assure you that I won't drink wine again until that day when I drink it in a new way in God's kingdom. (MARK 14:25)

10 Judas Iscariot, one of the Twelve, went to the chief priests to give Jesus up to them. 11 When they heard it, they were delighted and promised to give him money. So he started looking for an opportunity to turn him in.

12 On the first day of the Festival of Unleavened Bread, when the Passover lamb was sacrificed, the disciples said to Jesus, "Where do you want us to prepare for you to eat the Passover meal?"

13 He sent two of his disciples and said to them, "Go into the city. A man carrying a water jar will meet you. Follow him. 14 Wherever he enters, say to the owner of the house, 'The teacher asks, "Where is my guest room where I can eat the Passover meal with my disciples?"' 15 He will show you a large room upstairs already furnished. Prepare for us there." 16 The disciples left, came into the city, found everything just as he had told them, and they prepared the Passover meal.

17 That evening, Jesus arrived with the Twelve. 18 During the meal, Jesus said, "I assure you that one of you will betray me—someone eating with me."

19 Deeply saddened, they asked him, one by one, "It's not me, is it?"

20 Jesus answered, "It's one of the Twelve, one who is dipping bread with me into this bowl. 21 The Human One goes to his death just as it is written about him. But how terrible it is for that person who betrays the Human One! It would have been better for him if he had never been born."

22 While they were eating, Jesus took bread, blessed it, broke it, and gave it to them, and said, "Take; this is my body." 23 He took a cup, gave thanks, and gave it to them, and they all drank from it. 24 He said to them, "This is my blood of the covenant, which is poured out for many. 25 I assure you that I won't drink wine again until that day when I drink it in a new way in God's kingdom." 26 After singing songs of praise, they went out to the Mount of Olives.

"Plenty Good Room"

Refrain:
There's plenty good room, plenty good room,
Plenty good room in my Father's kingdom,
Plenty good room, plenty good room,
Just choose your seat and sit down!

Verse 1:
I would not be a sinner,
I'll tell you the reason why;
I'm afraid my Lord my call on me,
And I wouldn't be ready to die.

Verse 2:
I would not be a liar,
I'll tell you the reason why;
I'm afraid my Lord my call on me,
And I wouldn't be ready to die. (Repeat chorus)

Sit down! Sit down! Sit down!

Lenten Meditation

What does it feel like when your closest confidante reveals a secret about you to others, when your bestie/BFF does something to deliberately hurt you, when you need the help of a close friend who refuses to give it? Will there be room at your table for that person? Would you be able to sit down with her or him and share a meal? How do you handle betrayal?

We serve a God who makes room for us despite our daily betrayals. God makes room for us by providing the daily grace to do better than the day before. We have the assurance that there is plenty good room in God's kingdom for all betrayers, including you and me; for we know that we are one of the many for whom Jesus poured out his blood.

As we prepare the guest room of our hearts to receive a fuller meaning of Lent, let us ponder these questions. Through prayer, fasting, and Bible study, let us prepare our spirits to forgive others as God forgives us.

Prayer

Dear Lord, I want a seat at the table of your love. Prepare my heart, my mind, and my spirit. Help me to make room for all those to whom you offer your grace; in Jesus' name. Amen.

First Edition Notes
"Judgment and Death," page 41

While overtly referring to anticipated blessings in heaven, "Plenty Good Room" also had another message. Slaves were protesting their status in life where they were not given room to live, work, and exist as human beings. This state, as the words to the song clearly indicate, is not reflective of God's kingdom. In their "Father's kingdom" they had "plenty good room." The words of the spiritual were also a subtle protest against the tiny, one-room shacks and other deplorable lodgings in which the slaves were forced to live. Understandably, slaves longed for a place where they could have their basic physical needs met. As slaves, they physically and figuratively had no room.

Succeeding generations of African Americans extended their understanding of "Plenty Good Room" to include the equal participation of all persons at every level of society. African Americans were not given "room" to vote, work, shop, travel, or even eat equitably in the United States. Treated as members of the lower caste, they were systemically excluded from fully participating in societal life, even though they were citizens. The brutal victimization and disenfranchisement of blacks gave reason for many to despair. Spirituals like "Plenty Good Room," holy relics from the past, were dusted off and became reinvigorated symbols of the ongoing quest for human equality, even as the spiritual hope of the world beyond was maintained. This kind of activity characterized the Civil Rights Movement of the 1950s and 1960s.

Betrayal (Mark 14:10-11)

One of the differences in the social justice movements of the twenty-first century is that the younger generations are not dusting off the holy relics of the past or reinvigorating old spirituals and symbols. Emblazoned unapologetically on their T-shirts is "This Ain't Yo' Mama's Civil Rights Movement." Many reject the validity of the public display of forgiveness toward the killer demonstrated by those who lost family members in the 2015 Charleston massacre at Mother Emanuel AME Church. Students at elite universities were not merely trying to be included, asking for a seat at the table; they were going after the very structures of racism, calling for the removal of racist icons and administrators who just didn't "get it" in terms of structural racism. Football players even refused to play ball in support of those demands!

The spirituals that brought so much comfort and solidarity to the freedom fighters of yore have no meaning for these new warriors. Who can blame them? States have found different ways to keep young adults, people of color, and women from voting. Black children are being slaughtered in the streets and poisoned by water through homegrown terrorism. Police cover-ups of murders and wrongful imprisonments come to light almost daily. When these younger generations take to the streets in protest, they don't sing; they are not trying to out-love their oppressors. They feel betrayed by older generations, by the church, and by the system; and they want the oppression to stop!

They find the betrayal to be as deliberate as what Judas did to Jesus. They believe those who counsel cautiousness and politeness are merely playing into a system that has been rigged from the start. When Judas went to the chief priests, he was playing by their rules, and they were delighted. And like the money-lovers they were, they gave Judas money so that he could operate on the inside and find an opportunity to hand Jesus over.

Discussion Point
What is betrayal?

Preparing Room (Mark 14:12-16)

The Passover and the Festival of Unleavened Bread combine to make an eight-day event, commemorating the escape of the Hebrew children from the oppression of slavery in Egypt (Leviticus 23:4-8; Numbers 28:16-25). The Passover Seder (ceremonial dinner) occurs on the first day and sometimes the second day as well. It is a family and community event, with multiple generations in attendance. As with any big celebration, it must be prepared for, and Jesus had already put a plan in place for the disciples to carry out. They were to follow a man carrying a water jar. The place where he entered would be the house of their host who would show them a room large enough for their party. When the disciples followed his directions, they were able to prepare for the Passover meal.

Jesus has already made room for us.

> Don't be troubled. Trust in God. Trust also in me. My Father's house has room to spare. . . . When I go to prepare a place for you, I will return and take you to be with me so that where I am you will be too. (John 14:1-3)

How do we prepare room for him? During Christmas we sing, "Let every heart prepare him room" from the hymn "Joy to the World." All during the year we sing, "Lord, prepare me to be a sanctuary." A heart that is full of hatred and anger cannot be made ready for Christ or for anyone. When we remember that in this setting Jesus was on the way to be accused of and die for crimes that he did not commit, to suffer a cruel death at the hands of the state, and yet to sit down at the table with Judas, we realize that we can make room for him by following his directions.

When we follow what Jesus has told us, we can find the energy to grapple with the problems of the world with hearts of love and forgiveness. We must love our enemies and pray for those who persecute us (Matthew 5:44). And even as forgiveness is a process, we must ask God to give us room in our hearts to forgive.

> If you forgive others their sins, your heavenly Father will also forgive you. But if you don't forgive others, neither will your Father forgive your sins. (Matthew 6:14-15)

We can trust God, whose thoughts are higher than ours and whose plans are for our good. When we follow Jesus' directions, we will be led to a place where there is room for all.

Is It Me? (Mark 14:17-21)

Any parent of more than one child has had the experience of no one taking responsibility for some bad action. Who did it? "It wasn't me, Mommy!" "Not me!" "I didn't do it!" This was the same reaction of the disciples when Jesus made his announcement that someone would betray him. All were quick to deny culpability. Jesus' answer was interesting because the guilty included one of the Twelve, one who was sitting at the table eating with him, one who had dipped bread in the same bowl. Those descriptions covered them all.

This happens in our society. Who is responsible for the perpetuation of systemic racism? Have you done your part to diminish its effects? Or have you been complacent or even complicit? To be complacent is to be smug and uncritically satisfied about one's accomplishments. To be complicit is to participate in the wrongdoing. Too many African Americans became nonvigilant and complacent upon receiving the right to vote or being able to buy a house or car. However, as a group, except for the 2008 and 2012 presidential elections, we have low voter turnouts. Yet the bad loans of the 2008 economic downturn hurt black homeowners more than any other group. Black people need to remain engaged in local and regional issues from year to year in order to effect change that benefits everyone.

Those who would shut the door on affirmative action after having benefited themselves are complicit. There are those who look at the BlackLivesMatter (BLM) activists and wish that they would sit down, go back to class, get a job, forgetting that the same was said of the civil rights workers. They wish that the BLM movement was not so inclusive, forgetting that one of the mistakes of civil rights leaders of the sixties was to place women and strategist Bayard Rustin in the background and to be reluctant to form alliances with other oppressed groups like Native Americans and Hispanics. While the responsibility for dismantling white racism lies squarely on the shoulders of those who benefit most, we who are its victims must be careful not to follow its ways, just satisfied to sit at the table, rather than doing what we can to support those who have begun to shoulder the cross.

Discussion Point
What can you do to help to dismantle systems of oppression?

Transformation (Mark 14:22-26)

A seat at the table is not the goal. Judas was sitting at the table. Transformation and a new dispensation are the goals. A dispensation is a system of order. As the disciples participated in this familiar ritual they had performed their entire lives, Jesus transformed its meaning. No longer was the Passover meal just a ceremony of remembrance. Now it was a promise of things to come, "a new way in God's kingdom." It was the prelude to a new way of being, a new system of order, where the first would be last and the last would be first, and where those who had previously been on the margins were now fully included in the guest room.

As we move through this Lenten season, let us think about what transformation and a new dispensation might mean in our lives and in our society.

Discussion Points
How is Communion a means of grace by which our world becomes more like the beloved community Jesus bled and died for? What will it take to get there? How do we embody Christ in the world so that we make disciples who will do their part in a true transformation of the world and not create a mirror image of empires and systems that have reigned era upon era?

LESSON FIVE

✳ Ain't-a Dat Good News? Shouldering the Cross ✳

BIBLE LESSON: Matthew 27:27-37

KEY VERSE: As they were going out, they found Simon, a man from Cyrene. They forced him to carry his cross. (MATTHEW 27:32)

27 The governor's soldiers took Jesus into the governor's house, and they gathered the whole company of soldiers around him. **28** They stripped him and put a red military coat on him. **29** They twisted together a crown of thorns and put it on his head. They put a stick in his right hand. Then they bowed down in front of him and mocked him, saying, "Hey! King of the Jews!" **30** After they spit on him, they took the stick and struck his head again and again. **31** When they finished mocking him, they stripped him of the military coat and put his own clothes back on him. They led him away to crucify him.

32 As they were going out, they found Simon, a man from Cyrene. They forced him to carry his cross. **33** When they came to a place called Golgotha, which means Skull Place, **34** they gave Jesus wine mixed with vinegar to drink. But after tasting it, he didn't want to drink it. **35** After they crucified him, they divided up his clothes among them by drawing lots. **36** They sat there, guarding him. **37** They placed above his head the charge against him. It read, "This is Jesus, the king of the Jews."

"Ain't-a Dat Good News?"

Verse 1:
Got a crown up in-a dat Kingdom,
Ain't-a dat good news?
Got a crown up in-a dat Kingdom,
Ain't-a dat good news?

Refrain:
I'm a-gonna lay down dis world,
Gonna shoulder up-a my cross,

Gonna take it home-a to my Jesus,
Ain't-a dat good news?

Verse 2:
Got a harp up in-a dat Kingdom . . .

Verse 3:
Got a robe up in-a dat Kingdom . . .

Verse 4:
Got slippers in-a dat Kingdom . . .

Verse 5: Got a Savior in-a dat Kingdom . . .

Lenten Meditation

Life is full of contradictions, and a life following Christ is no exception. Take these words of Jesus, for example:

Come to me, all you who are struggling hard and carrying heavy loads, and I will give you rest. . . . My yoke is easy to bear, and my burden is light. (Matthew 11:28, 30)

A *yoke* is a collar used on beasts of burden. It is not easy or comfortable for them; they struggle against it. And a burden is called a burden precisely because it is heavy. Therein lies the contradiction; a yoke is not easy, and a burden is not light.

A cross is a burden, yet the enslaved ancestors, who knew something about heavy burdens, sang joyfully about lifting it onto their shoulders. As opposed to the contemporary need for instant gratification, they took the long view. They knew they had nothing, not even their own bodies, down here on earth. In making a decision to take up the cross of Christ and follow in his discipline, they exercised free will and exchanged a worldview of oppression for a kingdom perspective where God would eventually provide all that they needed. And that was good news!

Prayer
We thank you, Lord, for the heaviness of your message.

First Edition Notes

"Taking Up Our Crosses," page 31

We, like the slaves, have the opportunity to increase our understanding of what it means to take up our crosses and follow Jesus. What does it mean for us to "lay down this world"? Clearly we are called to be obedient and faithful to God; but can we say that the example of Christians today indicates a readiness to take up the cross for the gospel of Christ? Are we as assured as the slaves were about everlasting life and the presence of God in our lives?

"Crowns in the Kingdom," page 30

By choosing not to attempt to gain the world and therefore lose their lives, the slaves chose instead to place their hopes on life in Christ. Like Jesus, the slaves could shoulder up the cross of this world, the cross of affliction, and achieve the peace and assurance of a life with God.

Sticks and Stones, Crowns and Robes (Matthew 27:27-31)

One of the most erroneous sayings ever is, "Sticks and stones may break my bones, but words will never hurt me!" Parents have often taught children who are being bullied to hold this thought in their hearts. Children who are under constant threat of racial epithets know the untruth of it. How many fights have erupted over the horrible words that we have for others of a different race or faith, for those who wear different clothing, eat foods with an unfamiliar smell, or speak a different language?! How many teens have been prompted to commit suicide because they felt so different and were shamed and harassed by various methods? The scars left on the soul and psyche are unknown and immeasurable.

When Jesus was left in the hands of the governor's soldiers, he was tormented by words and by deeds. Surrounded by a company of men, he was stripped naked and raped by their eyes. He was mocked and humiliated. He was beaten and spat upon. The soldiers even caused harm to themselves by weaving a crown of thorns to place on Jesus' head. This was not the kind of crown about which the slaves sang. The soldiers placed on his shoulders one of their red coats as a "kingly" robe to signify that he was one with so-called power. They gave him a pretend scepter and knelt before him, derisively calling him king.

He committed himself to the LORD, so let God rescue him;
let God deliver him because God likes him so much.

(Psalm 22:8)

By their words and their actions, the soldiers' intent was to do damage, to break him down in his spirit, heart, soul, and mind. Lest we think that Jesus could not be affected by this behavior, let us remember that he was born of a woman, a human person with all of the characteristics of full humanity. This is how, even being fully God, he could die. It was not until they ran out of things to say that they took sticks and began to beat him in order to damage and break down his body, an easier task for one so dejected.

Insults have broken my heart. I'm sick about it. I hoped for sympathy, but there wasn't any; I hoped for comforters, but couldn't find any. (Psalm 69:20)

He was oppressed and tormented, but didn't open his mouth.

(Isaiah 53:7a)

Words hurt. Physical assault hurts. We should never think that the unkind things we say and do are not hurtful to those experiencing them. Ridicule, torture, and abuse are dehumanizing. Let us remember what Jesus said: "Truly I tell you, just as you did it to one of the least of these who are members of my family, you did it to me" (Matthew 25:40, NRSV).

When the soldiers had spent themselves making fun of Jesus, they stripped him naked again, removing the military coat. They put him in his own clothes and led him away to the place where the crucifixion would occur.

Discussion Point
What did you do when you were bullied?

Simon of Cyrene (Matthew 27:32-33)

While Cyrene (sigh-REE-nee) was a third-century BC Greek colony in Libya, Northern Africa, there had been a Jewish presence there from the time of King Solomon. In ancient times, the Jewish community maintained its ties with Jerusalem, with Cyrenians attending Jewish festivals (Acts 2:10). There was a significant Jewish population until the persecution of World War II, which continued through 1963, by which time most Jews had emigrated to Rome, Israel, or the United States.

Harlem Renaissance poet Countee Cullen (1903–1946) wrote a wonderful poem entitled "Simon the Cyrenian Speaks." It posits that Simon was chosen to bear Jesus' cross "because [his] skin [was] black." Cullen infers that Simon originally refused to do it, but the gleam he saw in Jesus' eyes bought his pity. He believed that Jesus was dying for a dream, and he made a decision to do "for Christ alone / What all of Rome could not have wrought / With bruise of lash or stone."[1]

Simon's presence in Jerusalem might have been due to the fact that it was Passover, a time of pilgrimage for every Jew. Why he was chosen was possibly a matter of convenience; he was standing in the road. Soldiers had the power to conscript and force anyone to serve their purposes at any time. The soldiers had brutalized Jesus so badly, he may have needed help on the uphill journey from the governor's house to Golgotha, a place outside of the city gates where anyone entering would see who was being punished and what crime they had committed. Its name had a gruesome meaning: "Skull Place."

Simon had two sons, Alexander and Rufus (Mark 15:21). Historically, Cyrene became an early center of Christianity. Cyrenians were among those who proclaimed Christ in Antioch. They were scattered from Jerusalem due to persecution, originally led by Paul (Acts 11:20). Nevertheless, there was a Rufus among the Christians in Rome to whom Paul sent greetings saying that he and his mother were outstanding believers (Romans 16:13). Perhaps Simon, their father and husband to their mother, had shared what he saw in Jesus when he carried his cross to the hill of crucifixion. When he shouldered the cross, whether by force or by choice, he took up the cause of Christ and spread the good news, first to his family, who then were evangelists throughout the Roman Empire. Aint-a that good news!

Discussion Point
Besides attending church, how do you spread the good news of Jesus Christ?

The Soldiers (Matthew 27:34-37)

Before Jesus was crucified, the soldiers offered him wine mixed with vinegar, which he chose not to drink. Wine vinegar is very bitter and offers no soothing or numbing alcoholic qualities. Offering it was part of the torture process. Once Jesus was affixed to the cross, apparently once again stripped naked, the soldiers divided his clothing according to how they had bet. Why would they want or need the bloody torn clothing of a prisoner? Why would taking bribes from poor people be part of their culture? This may speak to the economic status of the soldiers, what they were paid. John the

Baptist told Roman soldiers to be satisfied with their pay if they wanted to show their repentance (Luke 3:14). But here they are at Jesus' crucifixion, amplifying their goods with Jesus' rags! Corruption and violence have been part of police culture for thousands of years.

Twenty-first-century America is moving closer and closer to a model of militarized policing. While other nations focus on nonviolent arrest methods, rehabilitation, and emptying their prisons, America banks on recidivism and has a higher percentage of its people behind bars than any other nation. In 2015, prisoners like Freddie Gray in Baltimore and Sandra Bland in Texas found death while in the custody of the criminal justice system. Peaceful protesters have been greeted with armed trucks and riot gear. Prisons are run as for-profit institutions with guarantee from the state for ninety-percent-full population.[2] Even though not all in the criminal justice system take part, corruption runs from underpaid, undertrained police forces to judges who receive kickbacks for convictions.

Jesus was verbally brutalized as he went through his conviction process. He received a crown of thorns and a robe of humiliation. He was physically tortured. This scenario was not only played out again in slavery, but also in our present world when we saw Eric Garner (2014) choked to death by police on Staten Island, New York, or a fourteen-year-old girl in a bathing suit thrown to the ground with the knee of a policeman in her back (2015) at a pool party in McKinney, Texas. The slaves in their singing, however, could imagine how things would be turned around, that they would receive crowns and robes of glory. That is the challenge. The consecrated cross we must bear; there is a cross for you and for me. Like Simon, the cross we bear must lead to others choosing the way of the Lord!

Discussion Points
How do we shoulder the cross in a way that brings healing and transformation to the world? How do we continue to have hope that leads to joy "up in-a dat Kingdom" while never ignoring or neglecting the needs of this world?

1. From *The Bible and Its Influence*, edited by Cullen Schippe and Chuck Stetson (Fairfax, Virginia: BLP Publishing, 2006), page 224. See also *http://www.poemhunter.com/poem/simon-the-cyrenian-speaks/*.
2. See "How For-Profit Prisons Have Become the Biggest Lobby No One Is Talking About," by Michael Cohen, in *The Washington Post* (April 28, 2015), *https://www.washingtonpost.com/posteverything/wp/2015/04/28/how-for-profit-prisons-have-become-the-biggest-lobby-no-one-is-talking-about/*.

LESSON SIX
✳ Were You There?
A Collective Memory ✳

BIBLE LESSON: Mark 15:25-47

KEY VERSE: They crucified him. (MARK 15:24a)

25 It was nine in the morning when they crucified him. **26** The notice of the formal charge against him was written, "The king of the Jews." **27** They crucified two outlaws with him, one on his right and one on his left.

29 People walking by insulted him, shaking their heads and saying, "Ha! So you were going to destroy the temple and rebuild it in three days, were you? **30** Save yourself and come down from that cross!"

31 In the same way, the chief priests were making fun of him among themselves, together with the legal experts. "He saved others," they said, "but he can't save himself. **32** Let the Christ, the king of Israel, come down from the cross. Then we'll see and believe." Even those who had been crucified with Jesus insulted him.

33 From noon until three in the afternoon the whole earth was dark. **34** At three, Jesus cried out with a loud shout, *"Eloi, eloi, lama sabachthani,"* which means, "My God, my God, why have you left me?"

35 After hearing him, some standing there said, "Look! He's calling Elijah!" **36** Someone ran, filled a sponge with sour wine, and put it on a pole. He offered it to Jesus to drink, saying, "Let's see if Elijah will come to take him down." **37** But Jesus let out a loud cry and died.

38 The curtain of the sanctuary was torn in two from top to bottom. **39** When the centurion, who stood facing Jesus, saw how he died, he said, "This man was certainly God's Son."

40 Some women were watching from a distance, including Mary Magdalene and Mary the mother of James (the younger one) and Joses, and Salome. **41** When Jesus was in Galilee, these women had followed and supported him, along with many other women who had come to Jerusalem with him.

42 Since it was late in the afternoon on Preparation Day, just before the Sabbath, **43** Joseph from Arimathea dared to approach Pilate and ask for Jesus' body. (Joseph was a prominent council member who also eagerly anticipated the coming of God's kingdom.) **44** Pilate wondered if Jesus was already dead. He called the centurion and asked him whether Jesus had already died. **45** When he learned from the centurion that Jesus was dead, Pilate gave the dead body to Joseph. **46** He bought a linen cloth, took Jesus down from the cross, wrapped him in the cloth, and laid him in a tomb that had been carved out of rock. He rolled a stone against the entrance to the tomb. **47** Mary Magdalene and Mary the mother of Joses saw where he was buried.

"Were You There?"

Verse 1:
Where you there when they crucified my Lord?
Where you there when they crucified my Lord?
Oh! Sometimes it causes me to tremble, tremble, tremble.
Where you there when they crucified my Lord?

Verse 2:
Where you there when they nailed him to the tree?

Verse 3:
Where you there when the sun refused to shine?

Lenten Meditation

This song is one of lament in which African American slaves ask an existential question concerning an event at which their physical presence was impossible: "Were you there when they crucified my Lord?" However, anyone who had seen the brutal punishments of the era trembled in empathetic thought. Even as Billie Holiday grew up in the North (Philadelphia), she was able to sing hauntingly of the strange fruit on poplar trees in the South; and contemporary events such as the Charleston massacre of 2015 chillingly bring to the collective memory of black Americans cross burnings and lynchings of the not-so-distant past.

As we travel down the path to the cross, it is truly time to lament, to mourn, and to wail. Where are we? Why does this keep happening? We are trembling with grief, with dismay, and with fear. Others may await the terror beyond the borders, but we know that it has always been at our doorstep. Where are you, Lord? We are here.

Prayer
Walk with us, Lord, as we walk with you; in the name of Jesus. Amen.

First Edition Notes
"Justice and Equality," "Freedom Today," page 18

Throughout church and society, there are various roles and responsibilities persons assume in order to promote equality and dignity for all. Some are called to be clergy persons or politicians. Others are called to be activists who challenge systems of social, economic, and political oppression. This is particularly important in the case of the poor, African Americans, immigrants, and other ethnic groups who suffer disproportionately from the oppressive forces of poverty and economic exploitation, police brutality, unjust court systems, and sheer neglect in the United States.

Striving for equality for all oppressed persons is viewed as an issue of freedom. We must continue to ask ourselves how this theme may be applied to increasing levels of understanding deliverance for all humankind today.

The Crucifixion: Capital Punishment (Mark 15:24-27)

Christians often speak of crucifixion as if it only happened to Jesus—*my Lord*. In fact, it was the preferred extreme mode of capital punishment of the ancient world. In Latin, it means "fixed to a cross," but it was practiced from the ancient Persians all the way to the Britons. Thousands of people had their hands and feet fixed to a cross: "Were you there when they nailed him to the cross?" The cross was then hauled upright so that gravity could do its work of draining bodily fluids, dehydration, and asphyxiation.

Crucifixion was a death penalty for traitors and other criminals, of which Jesus was one. He, like the thieves on either side, was considered to be a threat to the peace of Rome—*Pax Romana*. It was used because it usually took so long for the crucified to actually expire—sometimes days. It took time for the sweat glands to rupture so that perspiration appeared as drops of blood; time for insects to lay eggs in the wounds, causing infection; time for all fluids to drain from the body or to pool in the abdomen, for the brain to begin to shut down and tell the heart and lungs to cease their function. Three centuries later, the Roman Empire outlawed crucifixion.

The carrying out of death penalties is public and necessarily cruel. Regardless of method, it is supposedly meant to act as a deterrent to crime. In the case of crucifixion, it was hoped that people passing by would look upon the spectacle and remember in some later desperate moment to refrain from stealing. Centuries later in the United States, in towns with prisons where the electric chair was used, townspeople knew the hour of an execution because of the surge on electrical capacity. Their lights dimmed; their radios cackled.

In the United States, death sentences cost taxpayers millions of dollars while the convicted go through the appeals process. With the advent of DNA testing, many convictions have been overturned. This means that in the past innocent people were executed. Christians may question why a so-called "Christian" nation would utilize the death penalty, realizing that it brought Jesus to his death. Jesus was innocent. Although the charge was that he claimed to be "king of the Jews," he had not committed treason as accused by his enemies. As he told Pilate, his kingdom was not of this world (John 18:36).

It was nine o'clock in the morning when they crucified Jesus (Mark 15:25).

Discussion Point
What are your feelings about the death sentence?

Were You There When They . . . ? (Mark 15:28-41)

They is often that vague term used to keep people anonymous. It is used to keep one's self blameless, as in "they said" or "they did it." Who is "they"? Who was there when Jesus was crucified? Here is a list of who they were and what they did:

1. Folk walking by casting aspersions and insults: "Ha!" "Save yourself!" (verses 29-30)
2. Chief priests and legal experts who knew how to twist the laws of Rome and of Moses to get the results they wanted: "He saved others, but he can't save himself!" (verses 31-32)
3. The thieves: "Save yourself and us!" (verse 32; Luke 23:39)
4. Some who thought he was calling on Elijah (verse 35)
5. Someone who ran to get him something to drink (verse 36)
6. The disciple whom he loved (John 19:26)
7. Women who had supported his ministry, including Mary Magdalene, Mary the mother of James and Joses, Salome, Mary the wife of Clopas, and Jesus' own mother and aunt (verse 40; John 19:25)

For the answer to the question of who crucified Jesus, the actual "they" refers to those who carried out the will of the Roman government. As maligned as Jewish people have been through history, they are not the ones who actually killed Christ. But they were there. Jesus was a member of the Jewish community. His haters and those who loved him were there.

Three Hours (Mark 15:33-47)

From noon until three o'clock in the afternoon, "the sun refused to shine." The literal darkness of Genesis 1:2 (it was dark over the deep sea), and the figurative/spiritual darkness that reigned before Jesus came into the world, returned.

> Though darkness covers the earth and gloom the nations, the LORD will shine upon you; God's glory will appear over you. Nations will come to your light and kings to your dawning radiance. (Isaiah 60:2-3)

As any child who is suffering, Jesus looked to his parent for relief and explanation. Using the words of Psalm 22:1, he cried out, "My God, my God, why have you abandoned me? Where are you?" It is the same question we ask in times of inescapable and inexplicable horror and grief, when a child is killed or arrested and sent to prison, when we or someone we love experiences rape and abuse, when communities are terrorized and families must flee persecution and irrational violence. We ask, "Where are you, God?"

When he died, the curtain of separation at the Temple supernaturally tore itself from top to bottom. By his sacrifice on the cross, Jesus removed the barriers between God and humanity, eliminating the need for a go-between priest and creating a priesthood of all believers.

> You yourselves are being built like living stones into a spiritual temple. You are being made into a holy priesthood to offer up spiritual sacrifices that are acceptable to God through Jesus Christ.
> (1 Peter 2:5)

The fact that it took Jesus only six hours to die and the way Jesus handled himself in the process convinced one soldier that Jesus was God's Son. As believers in Christ, how we live and die should lead others to have faith in Jesus Christ.

Discussion Point
How does the way a saint dies influence our faith in God?

When They Laid Him in the Tomb (Mark 15:42-47)

One of the last verses in the complete lyrics of "Were You There?" asks about our presence when Jesus was laid in the tomb. While no one reading this story today could have literally been there, we have all gone through burial rituals for loved ones. Timing is crucial. Black families usually allow more time between death and burial. Our families are far-flung due to migratory patterns, and folks need time to get off from work and find the money to get to the funeral.

For Jesus' community, the concern was that the work of burial could not be done on the Sabbath. They had to move quickly to bury Jesus before sundown, when the Sabbath would begin. Joseph of Arimathea asked Pilate for the body. After checking whether Jesus was actually dead (only six hours), Pilate gave his permission. Joseph lovingly wrapped the body in the traditional burial cloths and closed up the tomb with a stone while Mary Magdalene and Mary the mother of Joses watched. They were there when they laid him in the tomb.

This is where our journey during Lent ends, at the tomb. But it is not the end of the story! Life with God does not end in the graveyard. The dead places and spaces in the world are to be overcome by the light and life of God.

> The light shines in the darkness, and the darkness doesn't extinguish the light. (John 1:5)

As we await the celebration of Easter, let us meditate upon how we must move quickly to accomplish the work of bringing new life to a world so desperately in need of hope.

Discussion Point
How will you be a witness?

✳ LEADER GUIDE ✳

To the Leader

The Leader Guide will help you prepare in the facilitation and organization of the lessons for *Plenty Good Room* as you and your adult participants journey through the Lenten season. As mentioned in the preface, most material for this edition is brand-new, with even the songs being shared from two older Bible study resources, *Plenty Good Room* (2002) and *On Ma Journey Now* (2005). When you read the preface and introduction, you will gain an understanding of how and why this resource was put together.

THE MUSIC

Each lesson uses as its foundation not only a biblical text but an African American spiritual. For this reason it is critical to listen to each song and review the lyrics. Even if you have the first edition of *Plenty Good Room* and its CD, you will need to download the digital song files, using the link *http://www.abingdonpress.com/plentygoodroom*, because the song selections are different. The lyrics at the beginning of each lesson correspond to the downloads. However, you may also choose to have participants sing the songs. In this way we practice and pass along this oral tradition. Your devotional time may include

1. Listening to and/or singing the spiritual
2. Reading the key verse and Scripture lesson
3. Reading the meditation
4. Praying

THE BIBLE LESSON

This study is particular to the Lenten season, with an emphasis on preparing hearts to appreciate the great gift of Christ, our Passover, how he allowed his body to be broken and his blood poured out for the forgiveness of sins; and then to be ready to celebrate anew his resurrection, which gives us a right to the tree of life, life with our Lord forever! In the ancient church, it was a period wherein new converts were prepared for baptism. In many churches today, an Easter baptism is considered to be special, while other churches, including United Methodist, conduct confirmation classes during Lent with the goal of young people confirming their Christian faith on Easter Sunday. As you study, remember your own experience of growing

b. As the lesson proceeds, remind students of the key point made in these short paragraphs: that no matter our status in life, worship and song ushers us into the presence of God, with whom we are always connected.

3. *Place and Time (page 9)*
a. Assign students to read the passages mentioned in this section.
b. Give a brief summary of the miracles done through Moses (Exodus 17:5-7), Elijah (1 Kings 17:17-24), and Elisha (2 Kings 4:42-44).
c. In the discussion refer to the meditation for a definition of *theophany*.

4. *Theophany, Part I: What Did They See? (pages 9–10)*
a. Assign someone to read the Deuteronomy passage.
b. On a markerboard or flipchart, write down what the disciples saw (example: a shining, transformed Jesus, Moses, Elijah).
c. Discuss the importance of Moses and Elijah.

5. *Theophany, Part II: What Did They Hear? (pages 10–11)*
a. *Shema* is Hebrew for "Hear!" or "Listen!" In Jewish communities, the Shema is recited at the beginning and end of each day as an affirmation of faith in one God. When questioned about what is the greatest commandment (Matthew 22:36-40), Jesus quoted the Shema: to love God with all one's being. He also quoted Leviticus 19:18, to love one's neighbor as oneself, as the second most important commandment.
b. After having students review the three points of this encounter listed in the lesson, ask if there are more.

6. *Theophany, Part III: What Did They Do? (pages 11–12)*
a. In the iconic, foundational *Slave Religion: The "Invisible Institution" in the Antebellum South* (1978), Albert J. Raboteau begins with a poem from the Senegalese writer and veterinarian Birago Diop. One line is, "Those who are dead are never gone."[1]
b. As participants discuss what causes them fear, encourage them to think about the different aspects of fear: awe, respect, fright, terror.

7. *Coming Down the Mountain (pages 12–13)*
a. Discuss transformation. Have the participants reflect on how the Lenten journey can act as a guiding factor in connecting them to God.
b. Close the session in prayer.

LESSON TWO: This Lonesome Valley: A Time of Temptation

MATTHEW 4:1-4

KEY VERSE: Jesus replied, "It's written, *People won't live only by bread, but by every word spoken by God.*" (MATTHEW 4:4)

YOUR PREPARATION

1. Make every effort to increase your prayer time during this season.
2. Review the lyrics (page 14) as you listen to "Jesus Walked This Lonesome Valley."
3. Read the Scripture and meditation.
4. Think of a time when you experienced a "lonesome valley" (examples: a serious illness, a child's arrest and conviction, death of a parent or child, failure to pass an important test).
5. Read thoroughly and pray over each Scripture reference.
6. Review all directions and additional information. Choose which items you might share with participants when time permits.

DURING CLASS

1. Devotion

a. Have students open their books to page 14 and direct their attention to the lyrics. Play "Jesus Walked This Lonesome Valley," and invite participants to sing along.
b. Have the key verse and Scripture lesson read aloud.
c. Read silently the Lenten meditation.
d. Ask participants to think of a time when they experienced a "lonesome valley." You may choose to share yours. Allow time for them to share briefly.
e. Have the prayer read in unison.

2. First Edition Notes (page 15)

a. Before reading, inform participants that this section derives from the first edition of *Plenty Good Room* (2002), written by Lewis Baldwin.
b. As the lesson proceeds, remind students that lonesome valleys can be individual or communal, as in the slave experience.

3. Into the Wilderness (pages 15–17)

a. Take a moment for the group to think about the Hebrew meaning of the word *wilderness*.

b. The *Middle Passage* was the second leg of the transatlantic route wherein ships loaded with iron, brandy, weapons, and gunpowder first sailed from Europe to Africa. After selling these items, stolen human beings were loaded to be sold in the Americas. The final leg of the trade route was returning to Europe with goods from the Americas: sugar, cotton, tobacco, rum, and molasses. Slave ships could make three or four of these triangular routes per year.

c. As participants discuss the temptations they may face concerning food (addictive substances), position, and power, ask what they may need to do in order to be equal to the task.

4. Forty Days and Forty Nights (pages 17–18)

a. Lent always begins on a Wednesday, the day before being Mardi Gras or Fat (Great) Tuesday. Fat Tuesday meant cleaning out cabinets of white flour, sugar, and other edible temptations. People would have parties, sometimes known for physical and sexual excess. On Ash Wednesday, they would begin their fast, a time of abstinence from sinful behavior. The forty days before Easter exclude Sundays because Sunday is always a celebration of the resurrection of Jesus Christ, and there is no penitence or fasting. It is an opportunity to begin anew.

b. Ideas for Lent: (1) Give up electronics, social media, unhealthy foods or drinks. (2) Pray as you brush your teeth, hear an ambulance, before sending a text or e-mail. (3) Cultivate gratitude: Write thank-you notes, go out of your way to be kind to someone every day, donate money you've saved from frivolous purchases. (4) Read one chapter from the Bible daily, and share what you've read.

5. The First Temptation (pages 18–19)

a. As many as 52.5 million people in America, or seventeen percent, have low access to healthy food sources.[2] *Food deserts* are defined as urban neighborhoods and rural towns without ready access to fresh, healthy, and affordable foods.

b. Challenge participants to become more aware of the issue of food deserts. Use the USDA-ERS Food Desert Locator (*http://www.ers.usda.gov/data/fooddesert*) to view your area on a map. This online tool allows users to retrieve data on a county-by-county basis pertaining to food access.

6. Jesus' Response (pages 19–20)

a. Church should not be a lonesome valley or wilderness experience. Share these signs of church dysfunction with participants: (1) Severe theological errors and wrong biblical information are being taught. (2) High pastor turnover. (3) Unusual congregational conflict. (4) Church is invisible in the community; it is declining even though the community is growing. (5) Family-owned and operated. Ask participants if they know of other signs.

b. Healthy church members are critical in creating a healthy spiritual space for those who are not yet rooted. What lessons did the group learn in their personal wilderness experiences that can be helpful to strengthening others?

c. Close the session in prayer.

LESSON THREE: Bow Down on Your Knees: A Time of Repentance

MATTHEW 4:5-11

KEY VERSE: The devil left him, and angels came and took care of him. (MATTHEW 4:11)

YOUR PREPARATION

1. Make every effort to increase your prayer time during this season.

2. Review the song lyrics (page 21) as you listen to "Po' Mou'ner's Got a Home at Last."

3. Read the Lenten meditation and think about the meaning and character of angels. Where have you encountered them in the Bible? Some examples: Genesis 28:10-17; Numbers 22:22-35; Judges 13:2-6; 2 Kings 6:15-17; Luke 1:8-20. While more recent translations like the Common English Bible use the word *messenger*, older versions use the word *angel*, which from the Greek *angelos* means messenger. In addition to bringing messages, angels are believed to act as attendants and agents of God. Have you ever encountered an angel in your life?

4. Review all directions and additional information. Choose which items you might share with participants when time permits.

5. Read all additional Scripture passages thoroughly.

3. Betrayal (pages 29–30)

    a. Share from this list. Update the list; be aware of what else has happened since 2015.

- In 2015, student activists protested institutional racism at Harvard (Cambridge, Massachusetts), Tufts (Boston, Massachusetts), Princeton (New Jersey), Towson University (Maryland), Vanderbilt (Nashville, Tennessee), Michigan State, University of California at Berkeley, Stanford (California), Ryerson and the universities of Ottawa and Toronto in Canada.
- At the University of Cincinnati (Ohio), students called for police who were at the scene of a shooting of an unarmed black man to be barred from patrolling campus. [3]
- Across the country, some students demanded free tuition for black and indigenous students. Others demanded divestiture from for-profit prisons. [4]
- At Princeton, administrators removed the "masters" titles for heads of colleges, indicating that they were "historically vexed." Students also pushed for the removal of Woodrow Wilson's image and name from places of honor. From jobs to facilities, Wilson resegregated the federal government, undoing progress of Reconstruction, and promoted segregation and clan activity. *Birth of a Nation*, a 1915 film, was first shown in the Wilson White House. [5]
- In some cases, student agitation has been effective. In Nashville, after much unrest and legal action, Vanderbilt University determined to remove the word *Confederate* from the name of a dormitory, which is now known as Memorial Hall. It had been built in 1935 with money from the United Daughters of the Confederacy, a residence wherein female descendants studying education could live for free. After spending $10 million to renovate baseball facilities, students challenged Chancellor Nicholas Zeppos that the school could afford to return the 1.2 million required in order to change the name. On August 15, 2016, it was announced that the change would be made. [6]

    b. Have participants speak to the discussion point.

4. Preparing Room (pages 30–31)

    a. The Passover meal is preceded by a fifteen-part ritual service, the Passover Seder. *Seder* means "order" in Hebrew. Participants use a book, the Haggadah, to follow the order of service, which explains the importance of the foods as well as retells the Exodus story.

b. Discuss the nature of forgiveness and of making room for those who have betrayed us.

5. Is It Me? (pages 31–32)

   a. Bayard Rustin (1912–1987) was a civil rights and peace movement strategist, advisor to Martin Luther King Jr., and organizer of the 1963 March on Washington. His role was downplayed because he was gay. [7]

   b. Ask: How do oppressed people participate in oppression? Encourage them to find answers from the lesson. Move on to the discussion point.

6. Transformation (page 32)

   a. *Means of grace:* a way to experience God's love

   b. Offer an opportunity to engage the discussion points.

   c. Close this session in prayer.

LESSON FIVE: Ain't-a Dat Good News? Shouldering the Cross

MATTHEW 27:27-37

KEY VERSE: As they were going out, they found Simon, a man from Cyrene. They forced him to carry his cross. (MATTHEW 27:32)

YOUR PREPARATION

1. Make every effort to increase your prayer time during this season.
2. Review the song lyrics (pages 33–34) as you listen to "Ain't-a Dat Good News?"
3. As you read the Lenten meditation, think about the contradiction of an easy yoke and a light burden. Can you find examples in your life?
4. Read the entire lesson and all additional information. Choose which items you might share with participants when time permits.
5. Read all additional Scripture passages thoroughly.
6. Find an ancient map of Northern Africa, and identify Cyrene.

DURING CLASS

1. Devotion

   a. Have students open their books to pages 33–34 and direct their attention to the lyrics. Play "Ain't-a Dat Good News?"

b. Ask: How do you relate to the oppression of people who are different from you?

3. *The Crucifixion: Capital Punishment (pages 41–42)*

a. A new study of California's death penalty found that taxpayers have spent more than $4 billion on capital punishment since it was reinstated in 1978, or $308 million for each of the thirteen executions carried out since then. Calculations reveal that if the governor commuted the sentences of those remaining on death row to life without parole, it would result in an immediate savings of $170 million per year, with a savings of $5 billion over the next twenty years. The Florida Public Defender Association estimated that Florida spends $51 million a year to impose and implement the death penalty, rather than sending convicted first-degree murderers to prison for life without parole. It is estimated that each execution costs taxpayers $24 million.[9] The most rigorous cost study in the country found that a single death sentence in Maryland costs almost $2 million more than a comparable non-death penalty case. Before ending the death penalty, Maryland spent $186 million extra to carry out just five executions.[10]

b. These higher costs include the necessity to follow heightened due process, state-paid legal fees, expert witnesses, and strict imprisonment procedures. More than a dozen states have found that death penalty cases are up to ten times more expensive than comparable non-death penalty cases. Most costs associated with the death penalty never appear as line items in any budget. Instead, they are buried in a thicket of legal proceedings and hours spent by judges, clerks, prosecutors, and other agencies. In the time it takes to pursue just one capital case, law enforcement could investigate, prosecute, solve, and prevent scores of other crimes.[11]

c. Take time for the discussion point.

4. *Were You There When They . . . ? (pages 42–43)*

a. Assign someone to read each Scripture reference.

b. Challenge participants to imagine other "they's."

c. Ask: How do we kill Jesus every day?

5. *Three Hours (page 43)*

a. The Book of Psalms is the hymnal of Bible. Often, only the words of a hymn can describe or help our situation. Keeping in mind that some may not be familiar, have participants repeat this Charles Wesley hymn, line by line:

- Father, I stretch my hands to Thee.
- No other help I know.
- If Thou withdraw Thyself from me,
- Ah! whither shall I go?

   b. Have participants consider the significance of midday darkness and the characterization of "the sun refusing to shine."

6. *When They Laid Him in the Tomb (page 44)*

   a. Invite participants to talk about the funeral rituals practiced by their families: What is the wake like? Where do they have it (church, funeral home)? Is travel involved for family members? Is there food and storytelling?

   b. Include the discussion point and other comments.

   c. Close in prayer.

1. From *Slave Religion: The "Invisible Institution" in the Antebellum South*, by Albert J. Raboteau (New York: Oxford University Press, 1978), page 3.
2. See the Food Access Research Atlas, USDA Research Service, *http://www.ers.usda.gov/ data-products/food-access-research-atlas/documentation.aspx*.
3. See "University Students Hold Anti-Racism Protests Across US—As It Happened," by Jessica Glenza, in *The Guardian* (November 18, 2015), *https://www.theguardian.com/us-news/ live/2015/nov/18/studentblackout-anti-racism-protests-universities*.
4. See "Over 70 Black Campus Groups Plan More Protests, Demand 'Free Tuition for Black Students,'" by Jerome Hudson, on Breitbart (December 5, 2015), *http://www.breitbart.com/ big-government/2015/12/05/70-black-campus-groups-plan-protests-demand-free-tuition-black-students/*.
5. See "Wilson—A Portrait: African-Americans" on PBS, *http://www.pbs.org/wgbh/amex/ wilson/portrait/wp_african.html*. Also see "The Long-Forgotten Racial Attitudes and Policies of Woodrow Wilson" on the Boston University Professor Voices page, *http://www.bu.edu/ professorvoices/2013/03/04/the-long-forgotten-racial-attitudes-and-policies-of-woodrow-wilson/*.
6. See "Vandy's Black Students Put Zeppos on the Spot," by Jeff Woods, in *Nashville Scene* (November 17, 2015), *http://www.nashvillescene.com/news/pith-in-the-wind/article/13062092/ vandys-black-students-put-zeppos-on-the-spot*. Also see "Vanderbilt to Remove 'Confederate' From Building Name," by Adam Tamburin, in *The Tennessean* (August 15, 2016), *http:// www.tennessean.com/story/news/education/2016/08/15/vanderbilt-remove-confederate-building-name/88771680/*.
7. See Bayard Rustin's biography on Biography.com, *http://www.biography.com/people/bayard-rustin-9467932*.
8. See Countee Cullen's biography on Biography.com, *http://www.biography.com/people/countee-cullen-38950*. Also see his biography on Encyclopedia.com, *http://www.encyclopedia.com/topic/ Countee_Cullen.aspx*.
9. See "Costs of the Death Penalty" on the Death Penalty Information Center, *http://www. deathpenaltyinfo.org/costs-death-penalty*.
10. See "The Alarming Cost of the Death Penalty" on Equal Justice USA (EJUSA), *http://ejusa. org/learn/cost/*.
11. See *http://ejusa.org/learn/cost/*.

Abingdon Press™
Growing in Life, Serving in Faith

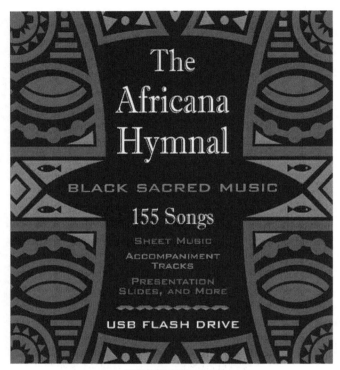

9781426795510

Black Sacred Music

A gift to hand down through the generations.
Everything you need to prepare and share all 155 songs
with your congregation on one USB flash drive.
Visit AbingdonPress.com/AfricanaHymnal
to hear samples of the songs.

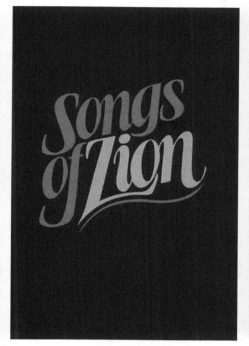

9781426795510   9780687335275

For Every Generation

Both songbooks include songs that have been part of the
African American worship tradition for many years and meant for
sharing in all worship settings.

Songs of Zion has:
Gospels | Spirituals | Benedictions | Chants | And more

In *Zion Still Sings* you will find:
African American spirituals | Black gospel | Traditional hymns
New hymns published in the 21st century | Urban rap | Hip-hop

Growing in Life, Serving in Faith

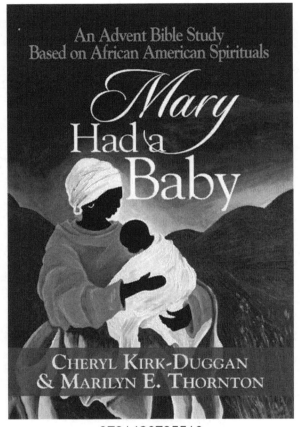

9781426795510

Also available in the African American Spirituals Collection
from Abingdon Press.

Learn the stories behind these beloved spirituals:
Mary Had a Baby
Rise Up, Shepherd, and Follow
Children, Go Where I Send Thee
Go, Tell It on the Mountain

Made in the USA
Las Vegas, NV
01 March 2022

44784441R00037